LEX POETICA : A Poetic Lore of Law & Jurisprudence

Vaibhav Surana

BookLeaf
Publishing

India | USA | UK

Presentation by *BookLeaf Publishing*

Web: www.bookleafpub.com

E-mail: info@bookleafpub.com

ISBN: 9789360943028

First edition 2024

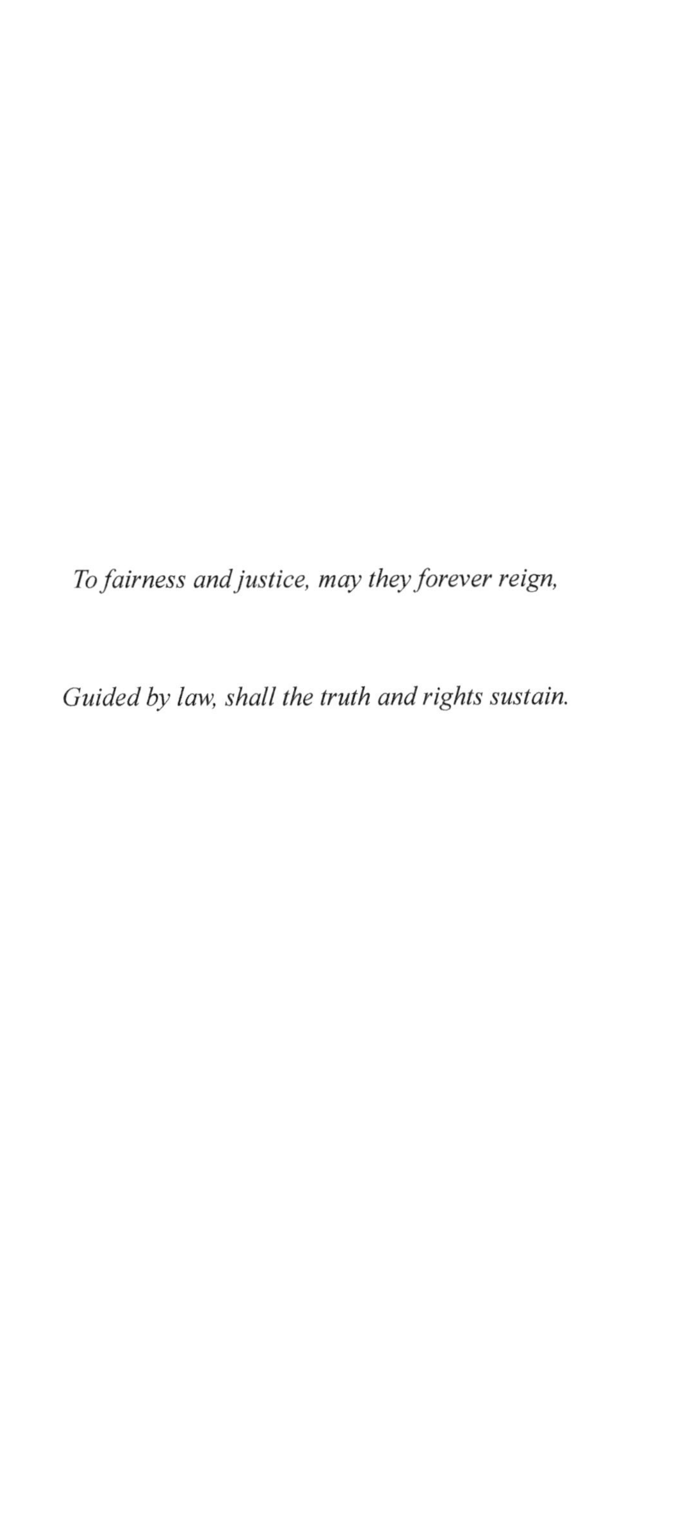

To fairness and justice, may they forever reign,

Guided by law, shall the truth and rights sustain.

LIST OF CONTENTS

Chapter 5: Double Jeopardy

A trial of errors leads Eldric to defend the principle
that one cannot be tried twice for the same offence.

Chapter 6: Privilege Against Self-Incrimination

Eldric faces coercion, championing the right to
silence in the face of incrimination.

Chapter 7: Right to a Fair Trial

A stranger's plight becomes Eldric's fight, ensuring
fairness in the judicial process.

Chapter 8: Habeas Corpus

Eldric challenges unlawful detention, advocating for
the freedom of the unjustly held.

Chapter 9: Proportionality

A lesson in the balance of justice, as Eldric, now
joined by Lena, confronts excessive punishment
being meted out to a youth.

Chapter 10: Judicial Independence

Eldric supports a judge under duress, emphasizing the
need for impartiality in justice.

Chapter 11: Ubi Jus Ibi Remedium

Seeking remedies for rights violated, Eldric and Lena
restore faith in legal redress.

Chapter 12: Stare Decisis

They delve into the power of precedent, guiding future decisions with wisdom from the past.

Chapter 13: Legal Capacity

Eldric champions the recognition of all persons to hold rights and responsibilities.

Chapter 14: Access to Justice

The duo breaks down barriers, ensuring justice is accessible to all.

Chapter 15: Audi Alteram Partem

Eldric and Lena advocate for the right to be heard, ensuring all voices contribute to the verdict.

Chapter 16: Nemo Judex in Causa Sua

Eldric and Lena present a challenge to the judge presiding over his own cause, thus promoting fairness in legal proceedings.

Chapter 17: Terra Nullius

Confronting historical injustices, they reclaim lands for those erased from history

Chapter 18: Actus Reus and Mens Rea

Exploring the complexity of intent and action in the commission of a crime.

Chapter 19: Lex Iniusta Non Est Lex

Eldric and Lena confront unjust laws, asserting that a true law must be just.

Chapter 20: Ignorantia Juris Non Excusat - Ignorantia Facti Excusat

A pivotal moment in understanding the nuances of ignorance in law and fact.

Chapter 21: Due Process

The cornerstone of Eldric's quest, advocating for fair treatment under the law. Eldric and Lena close this journey with a thumping victory.

Epilogue: The Legacy of Lex Poetica

Reflecting on the journey, Eldric and Lena's legacy is enshrined in the lore of law and justice.

Trivia

Some interesting information on the nomenclature of characters, the symbolism of words etc.

ACKNOWLEDGEMENT

In law's dense thicket,

Kind minds cleared the tangled paths-

Heartfelt thanks, my gift.

PREFACE

In the vast expanse where the disciplines of law and poetry seldom meet, "Lex Poetica: A Poetic Lore of Law & Jurisprudence" emerges as a confluence, a meeting ground enriched by the essence of both worlds. This book is born from a deep-seated belief in the power of narrative and verse to unravel the complexities of legal principles, making them accessible and resonant for all who seek understanding and wisdom in the realm of justice.

The genesis of this work lies in the observation that law, in its purest form, is a storytelling tradition. It is a compilation of narratives about society's values, conflicts, and aspirations. Similarly, poetry, with its rhythm and imagery, has the unique ability to distill vast concepts into their emotional and intellectual essence, connecting with the reader on a profound level. "Lex Poetica" is thus an experiment in blending these two venerable traditions to explore the terrain of jurisprudence through a new lens.

The journey you are about to embark upon with Eldric, our protagonist, is not merely a fantastical voyage through the mythical kingdom of Justicia. It is, more importantly, a pilgrimage through the landscape of law itself. Eldric's encounters, challenges, and revelations serve as allegories for the legal principles that underpin not just the fictional world of Justicia but our very reality. Each phase of his journey is a meditation on a fundamental legal concept, from the rule of law to due process, crafted to engage the reader's intellect and emotions in equal measure.

This book is designed for readers from all walks of life—students of law intrigued by the philosophical foundations of their discipline, lovers of poetry drawn to the narrative power of verse, and lay readers curious about the workings of justice in society. It is an invitation to explore how legal principles shape, and are shaped by the human condition.

Creating "Lex Poetica" has been a journey of discovery, not just in marrying the forms of law and poetry but in uncovering the universal truths that reside within legal doctrines. The process revealed that at the heart of every legal principle lies a story waiting to be told, a poem waiting to be written. It is my hope that this book will illuminate these truths for you, the reader, as it did for me, the author.

As we follow Eldric and Lena through their trials and triumphs, we are reminded of the enduring quest for justice that defines human societies across ages and cultures. Their story is a testament to the belief that law, at its best, is an instrument of fairness, equity, and righteousness. Through the medium of poetry, "Lex Poetica" seeks to celebrate this noble aspect of law, inspiring a deeper appreciation for the art and craft of jurisprudence.

Welcome to "Lex Poetica." May this journey enrich your understanding of law and ignite your passion for justice, as it has mine.

With sincere hope that these verses resonate with you,

VAIBHAV SURANA

PROLOGUE

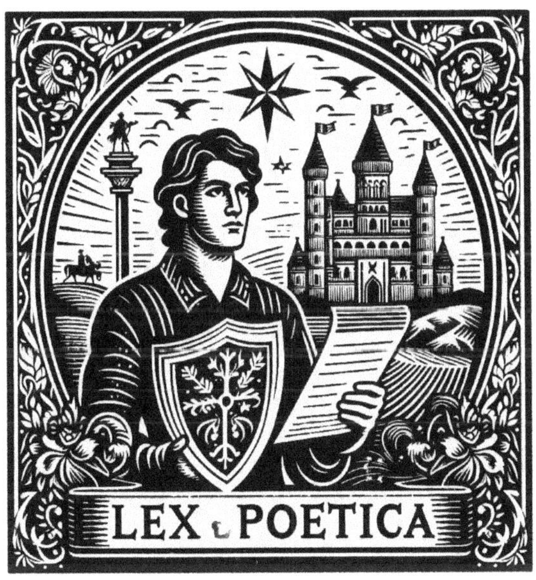

In a realm where pursuit of justice seemed heavy
and hard,
And laws enshrined spoke of battles marred,
One Eldric sets forth, with resolve in his core,
To right the wrongs of the lawless, to even the
score.

With parchment and purpose as his steadfast
shield,
Through courts and councils, he refuses to yield.

A journey begins, with the turn of a page,
Eldric steps forth, wisdom beyond his age.

With Lena, wise yet practical, joining his side,
Through trials and tales, they stride with pride.
From the rule of law to due process's gate,
Each step, a verse in the laws they debate.

"Lex Poetica," the lore of law and verse,
Not just a story, but a mirror to immerse,
Into the souls of those who dare to seek
The truth, the right, the just, for the meek.

Through principles twenty-one, a journey
unfolds,
In poetic verses, their story be told.
From ignorance of law, no excuse to find,
To fairness and equity, forever entwined.

In courts where the gavels ring clear,
Against tyrants and decrees, they stand without
fear.
For each law, a lesson, in each verdict, a song,
In Eldric's quest, righteous hearts grow strong.

So gather close, listen to the tale,
Of how perseverance and truth prevail.
In Justicia's lands, under wisdom's bright star,
Eldric's journey, through near and far.

Let the pages turn, let the verses flow,
As through Justicia's famed realms we go.
To learn, to reflect, to understand,
The power of law, in one Eldric's hand.

1. RULE OF LAW

In Justicia's land, where law once stood tall,
A decree was cast, that seemed unjust to all.
Lord Arbitrus, with power unchecked,
Banished one Eldric's kin, respect wrecked.

Eldric, a youth of spirit fierce and bright,
Stood against the darkness, a beacon of light.
With a tome in hand and justice in heart,
He vowed to play his part, to impart
The Rule of Law, a principle so divine,
Ensuring governance not by caprice, but line.

Through valleys deep and mountains high,
Eldric's journey under Justicia's sky
Was more than a quest for his family's name,
But a battle for all, to reclaim
The rights and laws unjustly seized
By a lord whose heart was far from pleased.

"Let the law be the guide, not the whim of one,
For justice under the sun, for everyone,"
Eldric cried out, his voice echoing far,
A call to arms, for those who bear
The weight of tyranny, the shadow of fear,
To stand up with Eldric, to draw near.

The Rule of Law, a foundation strong,
Ensures that to no one does power belong,
But distributed, checked, a balance of might,
It shall guide Justicia back to the light.
Eldric's quest, though fraught with strife,
Embarks with hope, for a better life.

Through every trial, every test,
Eldric's resolve would not rest.
For in his heart, he knew what's true:
That law is the guide, for me and you.
And so he marches, head held high,
Under Justicia's vast, unending sky.

To restore the Rule, to make right the wrong,
Eldric's path is brave and long.
But with each step, each deed so bold,
A new chapter of justice begins to unfold.
For in the land where law had fallen low,
Eldric seeks to let justice flow.

Thus begins the tale of a land reborn,
From the ashes of chaos, a new dawn.
With Eldric leading, the quest is clear:
To bring back the law, to all who are dear.
For justice, for freedom, for peace to reign,
In Justicia, where law shall govern again.

2. PRESUMPTION OF INNOCENCE

In the heart of a village, under suspicion's gaze,
Eldric found himself, in an unwelcome phase.
Accused of theft, a crime not his own,
In a place far from kin, standing all alone.

"No guilt is mine," he firmly declared,
With only his wit and his knowledge prepared.
"Innocence presumed," he recalled the law,
A principle of justice, firm and raw.

The villagers watched with eyes of doubt,
As Eldric stood firm, his voice strong and stout.
"Not guilty until proven," he did insist,
A shield of virtue in a clenched fist.

He sought out the truth, with logic and grace,
Challenging evidence, giving chase.
For in Justicia, where shadows may lie,
The light of innocence must never truly die.

The real thief, hidden amongst the fold,
Watched as the story of truth unrolled.
Eldric's determination, his unwavering quest,
Brought forth the truth, put to the test.
With innocence proven, the village saw,
The strength of the law, without flaw.
Eldric's name cleared, his spirit unbound,
In the principle of innocence, justice he found.

From this trial, a lesson was learned:
The flame of fairness cannot be burned.
For every soul, until guilt is shown,
Stands innocent, their virtue not overthrown.

Eldric's resistance, through doubt and fear,
Illuminated the path, made the way clear.
For where false accusations would fly,
The presumption of innocence must never die.

Onward he traveled, with justice in sight,
A victory in darkness bringing some light.
For Eldric knew, with each challenge he faced,
In the heart of the law, innocence is first
embraced.

Thus, the tale of Eldric begins to grow bright,
A beacon of hope in the endless night.
With the presumption of innocence as his guide,
He journeys forward, with justice by his side.

3. EQUALITY BEFORE LAW

After innocence was proven, Eldric took to the road,
His heart lighter, yet mindful of the code.
The next chapter of his journey did unfold,
In a village where the truth had yet to be told.

There he met Lena, whose voice was small,
Facing injustice, her back against the wall.
Discrimination faced, for her status and name,
A common plight, a pervasive game.

"Oh Eldric," she pleaded, "stand with me,
For in Justicia, surely all can be free.
Yet here I stand, unequal before the law,
My rights diminished, my hope so raw."

Eldric listened, his resolve took flight,
For Lena's cause was just and right.
Together they stood, a testament to the fight
For equality in law's unyielding light.

"Before the law, none shall stand above,
For justice sings the song of equal love.
And so equality we shall demand,
together we'd band, across this land."

In the court, they made their stand,
Eldric and Lena, together, hand in hand.
He spoke of laws from ages past,
Of equality and rights that must last.

"The law," he declared, "is a shield for all,
Not just for the mighty, the rich, or those tall.
But for every soul, in this land so wide,
Equality before the law, our constant guide."

The judges pondered, their hearts were swayed,
By the eloquence of the case Eldric made.
In the end, justice rang true and clear,

Equality before the law, for all to hear.

Lena's victory was more than her own,
A step towards a future where justice is sown.
For in Justicia, where Eldric roams,
Equality before the law, in hearts and homes.

So on he travels, on his own for now, but with
stories to tell,
Of Lena, of justice, of breaking the spell.
For in each tale, a lesson so bright,
Equality before the law, our eternal light.

Eldric's journey, far from done,
Underneath the same bright old sun.
With each step, his legend grows,
Wishing well that the law equally flows.

4. LEGAL CERTAINTY

From the village where equality's light shone
bright,
Eldric journeyed forth, into the long winding
night.
A town ahead, where laws shift like sand,
A place of chaos, far from justice's hand.

Here, people lived in perpetual fear,
Uncertain of the law, both far and near.
"Legal Certainty," Eldric thought, "must be
restored,

For without it, justice is but a broken chord."

He spoke to the townsfolk, gathered in the
square,
Of a world where the law is clear and fair.
"A stable law, like a lighthouse in the storm,
Guides us all, and keeps us from harm."

With patience and zeal, Eldric began to teach,
Of the principles of law, he aimed to breach
The walls of doubt, the clouds of dismay,
Lighting a path to a brighter day.

"Let's draft new laws," he proposed with care,
"Clear, steadfast, and utterly fair.
Laws that stand firm, like ancient trees,
Offering shelter, a gentle breeze."

The townsfolk rallied, inspired by his word,
Their voices united, their spirits stirred.
Together they toiled, from dawn till dusk,
In Eldric's wisdom, they placed their trust.

The new laws were crafted, a testament to hope,
A beacon of certainty, a vast and noble scope.
"Legal Certainty," they declared with pride,
"In our town, it forever shall reside."

As Eldric departed, the town anew,

He left behind a lesson, eternal and true.
That laws, like the stars, should steadfastly shine,
Guiding us forward, line by line.

And so Eldric's journey, a tale of light,
Continues onward, against the night.
With Legal Certainty his banner unfurled,
He ventures forth, to enlighten the world.

5. DOUBLE JEOPARDY

With Legal Certainty's beacon set alight,
Eldric journeyed on, his heart ever bright.
Yet soon he found, in a hamlet serene,
A shadow of a past trial, unjust and unseen.

Accused once more, for a past allegation,
A test of law, in justice's tribulation.
"Double Jeopardy," the principle clear,
Once judged innocent, no more to fear.

"Twice tried for one crime? This cannot be,"
Eldric proclaimed, "Let justice see.

For the law states, in its wise decree,
No soul shall face the same trial, once free."

The accuser, emboldened, with malice afresh,
Sought Eldric's downfall, their conflicts enmesh.
But Eldric stood firm, with law as his shield,
Determined that truth would soon be revealed.

He gathered the townsfolk, in the square they
met,
To speak of a law, lest any forget.
"A trial once concluded, its verdict cast,
Shall stand immutable, from first to last.

No second trial shall tread the same ground,
Once innocence or guilt has been found.
This is our right, under the sky so vast,
A safeguard from shadows, from accusations
past."

With eloquence, Eldric pleaded his case,
In the court of public opinion, he found his
place.
The principle of Double Jeopardy, his newest
guide,
Against the tides of accusation, he did abide.

The accuser's attempts, all drama to no avail,

For justice once served, unless appealed shall
ever prevail.
The townsfolk saw truth, in Eldric's plea,
The shadow of the past, now set free.

Eldric's name was cleared, once again to roam,
With Double Jeopardy's shield, he found his way
home.
"Justice has spoken," he said with a sigh,
"Under Justicia's watchful eye."

So Eldric's saga, with wisdom imbued,
Through trials and triumphs, is continually
renewed.
With each principle, a lesson sown,
In the heart of the law, justice grown.

Double Jeopardy's tale, a notion of right,
Guides Eldric onward, through another night.
For in Justicia, where his journey treads,
The law is an ally, a sheltering shed.

6. PRIVILEGE AGAINST SELF-INCRIMINATION

Through hamlet and field, Eldric's journey
wove,
Bearing lessons of law a treasure trove.
Yet in a twist of fate, under the cloak of night,
Bandits seized him, a victim of plight.

Bound and questioned, under threat's grim
shadow,
They sought confessions, deep and shallow.
"Speak!" they demanded, "Admit your crime,

Or suffer we promise, 'til the end of time."

But Eldric, undaunted by fear or blade,
Recalled the law's shield that never would fade.
"The Privilege Against Self-Incrimination,"
He declared, "Is my resolute proclamation."

"No word shall pass my lips, to aid your scheme,
For the law protects, even in a dream.
I shall not be compelled, against myself to
testify,
Under Justicia's gaze, beneath her sky."

The bandits sneered, yet Eldric affirmed,
With knowledge of law, steadfast and firm
"Forced confessions, under duress and pain,
Shall not stand in court, they're void and vain."

With courage and wisdom, Eldric held tight,
To the principles of law, through the darkest
night.
And as dawn broke, the bandits' resolve thinned,
Realizing the battle, they could not win.

Released at last, Eldric continued his quest,
Each trial faced, a formidable test.
But with law as his compass, and justice his aim,
Each challenge surmounted, added to his fame.

"Privilege Against Self-Incrimination," a right so
profound,
Ensures silence is golden, when danger's around.
Eldric's journey, a testament to this creed,
In a world where the law is the highest deed.

So on he walks, through Justicia's vast lands,
Defending the innocent, with unwavering hands.
For in each heart, and in every nation,
Lies the sacred right against self-incrimination.

7. RIGHT TO A FAIR TRIAL

Having averted danger, with freedom anew,
Eldric's path led him to a curious milieu.
In a town where the scales of justice were blind,
A stranger's plight caught his discerning mind.

Accused, yet innocent, in the public's eye,
Without a defender, under Justicia's sky.
Eldric stepped forward, his purpose clear,
To uphold the law, dearer than any spear.

"The Right to a Fair Trial," he proclaimed,
"Is a cornerstone of justice, unashamed.
Each soul deserves a chance to stand,
And plead their case, in this land."

He stood by the stranger, in the court's grand
hall,
Where the echoes of justice did solemnly fall.
With logic and passion, Eldric made the case,
For fairness, for truth, in this crucial space.

He argued for evidence, for witnesses to speak,
For the law to protect both the strong and weak.
"A fair trial," he said, "is not merely a right,
But the very essence of justice's light."

The judges listened, as Eldric's words took
flight,
Challenging the darkness, with law's might.
And as the verdict was read, under the weight of
truth,
The stranger was freed, his innocence the proof.

The town rejoiced, for justice had been done,
Thanks to Eldric, whose journey had only just
begun.
For the Right to a Fair Trial, he had shown,
is a pillar of law, steadfast and known.

Eldric's quest, a hymn of hope and trial,
Filling the bowl of truth vial by vial.
For in his heart, and through his deeds,
He plants the seeds of justice, tending to its
needs.

And on Eldric travels, with the law as his guide,
Through Justicia's lands, wide and wide.
With the Right to a Fair Trial, a done old deed,
He ventures forth, where the call of justice leads.

8. HABEAS CORPUS: Bring Forth The Body

Beyond the town where fairness won the day,
Eldric wandered, through mists and skies of
gray.
A fortress loomed, where whispers spoke of
dread,
Of prisoners taken, their fates hanging by a
thread.

In the shadow of stone, without trial or charge,
Detained in silence, their world small and dark.

"Habeas Corpus," Eldric thought, his heart
ablaze,
"The right to challenge detention, through the
maze."

Within the knowledge of a court, he approached
the fortress gate,
Confronting the guard, the hour growing too
late.
"Bring forth the jailed, let them see the light,
For none should be held, without justice in
sight."

The guard stood silent, the keys heavy in hand,
But Eldric's resolve was a firm demand.
Through corridors cold, to the dungeons deep,
Where hopes dwindle, and sorrows seep.

One by one, the prisoners were brought to the
day,
Blinking in sunlight, as Eldric led the way.
"To court," he declared, "where the matter will
be heard,
For Habeas Corpus is our sacred word."

Before the judges, Eldric made his stand,
For each soul present, he lent his hand.
"Let them speak, let their stories unfold,
For justice in silence is justice untold."

The court was stirred, by Eldric's plea,
For the essence of freedom, is being allowed to
be.
And as the judges listened, their hearts were
swayed,
By the power of law, Eldric had displayed.

One by one, the charges were brought to light,
And one by one, justice took flight.
For those wronged, freedom was regained,
In Habeas Corpus, their rights sustained.

The fortress, once a place of total despair,
Now stood relatively empty, its halls bare.
For Eldric had shown, through courage and
might,
That in the darkness, there can be light.

And yet again Eldric goes on with tales anew,
Of Habeas Corpus, and the freedom it drew.
For in the fight for justice, every victory counts,
In the balance of law, every moment amounts.

Through lands near and far, Eldric hath roamed,
A guardian of law, in the stories here poemed.
For where the call of justice begins to chorus,
There you'll find Eldric, and the spirit of Habeas
Corpus.

9. PROPORTIONALITY

In a hamlet shadowed by an ancient oak's
sprawl,
Eldric had just arrived, heedful of justice's call.
A tale of woe had found its way,
A harsh decree that led astray.

A youth, once buoyant, now bore a chain,
For a trifle misstep, the punishment insane.
"For a loaf of bread, a price too steep,
A life now in ruins, a family in weep."

Eldric's heart, firm and resolute,
Knew well the path, the absolute.
Essence of justice, its core, its root,
Proportionality here, was in certain dispute.

"Let us gather," Eldric's voice did soar,
"By this oak, let justice restore.
For laws are not chains, but shields in hand,
To guard, to guide, through any quicksand."

The townsfolk assembled, their eyes alight,
As Eldric spoke into the night.
"Proportionality," he began, "a scale so true,
Balances the deed with the appropriate due."

A murmur arose, a collective sigh,
As the moon climbed silently high.
Eldric, with fervor, painted the sky
With words of justice, pure and nigh.

Then from the crowd, stepped forth a familiar
face,
Lena, her spirit filled with hope and grace.
"Once more," she said, "I stand in this place,
Where justice seeks its rightful space."

Together they stood, a force combined,
Eldric's wisdom and Lena's mind.
They argued for fairness, for punishment kind,

For the youth's future, not to be confined.

As dawn broke, the verdict anew,
The scales of justice, balanced and true.
A sentence fair, with a future in view,
The village rejoiced, as hope flew.

The youth, now grateful, with eyes so bright,
Thanked Eldric and Lena, under the morning
light.
"For proportionality," he whispered, "A
welcome right,
In calls for justice, when none in sight."

Eldric smiled, his journey now vast,
Each victory sweet, none the last.
For in the tale of justice cast,
Proportionality held the main mast.

With Lena at his side, through lands they shall
roam,
Spreading the word, let law be known.
For justice is a garden, forever grown,
Needs hands to tend, so the fruits be shown.

10. JUDICIAL INDEPENDENCE

Beyond the hamlet, through gorge and glen,
Eldric and Lena had just heard then,
Where some rumours told of a judge's plight,
Bound by shadows, far from light.

In a town where the gavel's sound
Was drowned by power, tightly bound.
A judge once fair, now lost his way,
Under pressure's thumb, his judgments sway.

"The heart of justice," Eldric spoke,
"Must stand alone, its truth evoke.
Judicial Independence, a sacred cloak,
Ensures the law is never broke."

Together they planned, under star's soft gleam,
To restore the balance, to redeem
The judge from chains of influence dire,
To reignite fair justice's fire.

With dawn's first light, they made their stand,
In the town square, bold and grand.
"Evidence we bring," Eldric proclaimed,
"Of justice's path, wrongfully blamed."

Lena's voice, clear and strong,
Joined Eldric's call, a rallying song.
"For a judge to see, with eyes unclouded,
Is a principle upon which justice is founded."

The townsfolk gathered, their chatter grew,
As the judge listened, his conscience anew.
The chains of pressure, of fear and of might,
Began to loosen, in justice's light.

With each word, each plea, each cry,
The judge found again his purpose high.
"To judge with independence, to hold the line,
Ensures justice pure, through time."

The gavel fell, its sound so clear,
Echoed through the square, for all to hear.
A declaration, a vow to keep,
Judicial Independence, a trust so deep.

The judge stood tall, his path correct,
His judgment fair, his court earned respect.
Eldric and Lena, their mission complete,
Witnessed justice's heart, once more upbeat.

As they left the town, under a sky wide and blue,
Their spirits lifted, their bond anew.
For in the quest for justice, every victory shared,
Is a testament to the belief they both bared.

Through every trial, through every test,
Eldric and Lena, together, must conquest.
For Judicial Independence, they would attest,
In a world of law, it stands the best.

11. UBI JUS IBI REMEDIUM: Where There's A Right, There's A Remedy

From the town where justice found its voice
anew,
Eldric and Lena, through lands of morning dew,
Journeyed forth, their spirits high,
Beneath the vast, unending night sky.

In a village gripped by silent cries,
Where the weak met not justice's eyes,

A principle awaited, its call to rise,
"Ubi Jus Ibi Remedium," as say the wise.

Here, the people's pleas went unheard,
Their rights dismissed, justice deferred.
Eldric listened, his heart stirred,
By tales of woe, and its every word.

"In every right, a remedy must dwell,
For justice's garden to truly swell.
Where there's a wrong, we must compel,
justice to act, its power to tell."

Lena watched Eldric, saw the change,
His resolve hardened, he sought to arrange,
the justice scattered, his aim to rein.
The fabric of law, its scope to explain.

Together, they gathered in the village square,
Eldric's voice rang clear, far and fair,
"For every right infringed, let's dare,
To seek remedy, justice to repair."

With Lena's support, her keen insight,
Eldric argued with all his might.
"For justice to thrive, to reach its height,
Remedy and right must align in light."

The villagers mustered, their courage newfound,

In Eldric's words, a miraculous rebound.
Call to action, a binding sound,
Ubi Jus Ibi Remedium, ever so profound.

The local magistrate, once blind to pleas,
Now had to yield, as he felt the squeeze
Of justice's grip, its power to seize,
The heart of law, with ample ease.

Remedies granted, rights restored,
The village found its harmonious chord.
Justice's balance, once more adored,
Eldric's wisdom, had been the villagers' sword.

As they departed, the village aglow,
Eldric felt a growth, although slow
But sure, within his soul's flow,
A deeper understanding, a conquered plateau.

For every step, every right defended,
Eldric's spirit, further ascended.
Ubi Jus Ibi Remedium, now comprehended,
On this journey, justice be extended.

With Lena still along, a partnership rare,
Together they showed, how much they care.
For justice's path, they did prepare,
With every challenge, ready to dare.

12. STARE DECISIS: Follow The Precedent?

Beyond the village, where rights found their day,
Eldric and Lena trotted 'neath clouds a little
grey.
A crossroad came, where paths of law entwine,
Leading them to a challenge, by design.

In a town where precedent's shadow cast long,
Decisions past, both right and wrong,
Guided the present, a continuous song,
"Stare Decisis," where beliefs belong.

Here, a dispute, old as the stone,
Between neighbors, over boundary lines grown.
Each cited cases, in tones overblown,
Seeking to claim the truth as their own.

Eldric pondered, beneath an ancient tree,
How law's history shapes what will be.
"Stare Decisis," he mused, "a vast sea,
Guiding us through eternal continuity."

With Lena's advice, a plan took form,
To navigate through this legal storm.
In the town hall, they stood to inform,
On how precedents may transform.

"Let's look to the past, with eyes anew,
For lessons learned, and insights true.
But not be blinded, by the view,
For justice evolves, and law does too."

Eldric spoke of cases, old and wise,
Of how law grows, and never dies.
Yet, urged caution, to amply realize,
Blind adherence, was to justice's demise.

The townsfolk listened, drawn to the tale,
Of law's journey, a vast, winding trail.
With every precedent, set to sail,

Towards a future, where justice will prevail.

The dispute eventually resolved, with past in
hand,
A fair decision, for both parties' land.
"Stare Decisis," a guide so grand,
Yet flexible, to suit justice's demand.

As Eldric and Lena left the town,
Their spirits lifted, although never down.
For in each challenge, they found renown,
And law's beauty, their jeweled crown.

Stare Decisis, a thread through time,
Connecting the past, to the current climb.
Eldric's journey, a rhythm, a rhyme,
With Lena's support, now sublime.

Through every town, every lesson learned,
Towards justice, their hearts yearned.
With Stare Decisis, the past discerned,
And the future of law, brightly burned.

13. LEGAL CAPACITY

Beyond the town where past and present blend,
Eldric and Lena's path took a sharp bend.
To a village stuck in an age-old blight,
Where some were shadowed, denied their legal
light.

"Legal Capacity," Eldric pondered, "a right to all
bestowed,
Yet here lies a tale, where justice's march is
slowed.
Every soul deserves a voice to be heard,
A place in the court, their rights assured."

In this hamlet, certain folks were unseen,
Their voices muted, as if they'd never been.
Lena, with a spark in her gaze, did declare,
"It's time for change; it's only fair."

They gathered the village, under a temple's
grace,
Eldric and Lena, standing face to face
With those long silenced, now eager to share,
Their stories, their dreams, in the open air.

"With legal capacity," Eldric's voice rang true,
"Each person's rights come into view.
No longer shadows, but figures whole,
With the power to act, to claim their role."

They spoke of a law, where each voice could
thrive,
A new decree, to bring justice alive.
To recognize all, with no exception,
In legal matters, to have direction.

Lena worked beside, her wisdom like a torch,
Guiding the drafting, on justice's porch.
Together, they wove a tapestry of law,
Where every individual could their rights draw.

The village council, moved by the plea,

Voted to change, to set the decree free.
"Legal capacity for all," they echoed, a new
dawn to see,
Where every soul's rights would be guarantee.

As the decree was announced, under the sun's
glaring eye,
Joy and relief, as a cool breeze blew gently by.
Eldric and Lena, in the heart of the throng,
Felt the pulse of justice, steady and strong.

"Today," Eldric said, "we've seen a new start,
Where legal capacity plays its part.
Not just a privilege for the few to claim,
But a universal right, in justice's name."

With the village behind them, a beacon of
change,
Eldric and Lena continued, across the range.
For each victory in law, another step to the crest,
In their quest for justice, without much rest.

Legal capacity, a fundamental key,
In the journey of justice, as vast as the sea.
With hearts emboldened, and spirits high,
Eldric and Lena's aims soared to the sky.

14. ACCESS TO JUSTICE

Through valleys deep and mountains sheer,
Eldric and Lena, companions now dear,
Came upon a crossroads, where the air was cold,
A village hidden, with sad stories untold.

"Access to Justice," the cry went up,
From the lips of the weary, an empty cup.
But how to quench this thirst so deep,
When the climb to justice was so steep?

Eldric pondered, his mind set on course,
"Every soul should have proper recourse,

To seek redress, to claim their right,
In the broad daylight or the quiet of night."

Lena paused, her thoughts adrift,
"Yet, not all paths to justice are very swift.
Some are tangled, some are long,
And some, dear Eldric, may lead us wrong."

Herein lay a rift, a divergence of view,
Between two hearts, both steadfast and true.
Eldric sought the broadest possible gate,
While Lena warned of paths dictated by fate.

"Should not wisdom guide the way,
Lest our haste leads us astray?"
Lena proposed with a gentle tone,
Her words not a challenge, but a cornerstone.

Eldric listened, his respect undimmed,
For in Lena's caution, wisdom brimmed.
"Together, let's forge a path that's clear,
One that brings justice near, without fear."

In unity, they turned to the task,
Proper access to justice, was all they asked.
They worked with the villagers, side by side,
To build a path possibly most wide.

Legal clinics, they helped to found,

Where the voice of justice could resound.
And workshops, too, where knowledge was
shared,
So in their own defense, each could be prepared.

Lena's wisdom, like a beacon shone,
Guiding their efforts, till the day was done.
Eldric's passion, a flame so bright,
Illuminated the path through the darkest night.

The village found its way to the light,
With access to justice, their future bright.
Eldric and Lena, briefly at odds,
Discovered that together, they could defy the
gods.

For in their debate, a truth was revealed,
That through mutual respect, wounds could be
healed.
And in their journey, a lesson so grand,
That together, there's no challenge they can't
withstand.

"Access to Justice," now slightly warmer
Spread by Eldric and Lena, throughout this
corner.
For where paths converge, in the heart of the
fray,
There lies the strength, to light the way.

15. AUDI ALTERAM PARTEM: Hear The Other Party

In lands where the whispering winds sway,
Eldric and Lena now found their way
To a city divided, where silence reigned,
In courts where only one side explained.

"Audi Alteram Partem," Eldric recalled,
"Let the other side also be called.
For prudence to be true, and to be just,
Hearing both sides is an absolute must."

Yet, in this place of marble and stone,
The scales of justice were overthrown.
One voice dominated, loud and clear,
While the other whispered, drowned in fear.

Lena observed, with a furrowed brow,
"This imbalance, we cannot allow.
For every story has two sides,
In every truth, some justice resides."

Together, they approached the city's gate,
Determined to challenge this twisted fate.
"With wisdom and patience, we'll make them
see,
The robustness of our motto, however hard it
may be."

They called upon the elders, wise and revered,
Presenting a case that had to be heard.
"Let voices rise, both old and new,
For justice to be fair, to be true."

Eldric spoke of ancient times,
When justice was served by the ringing of
chimes.
"Audi Alteram Partem, a principle so old,
In its wisdom, a story told."

Lena, with grace, took up the plea,

"Imagine a world where all are free
To speak, to argue, to defend,
Where every voice can ascend."

Moved by their passion, even the meek stirred,
From every corner, voices started to be heard.
A council was called, under the open sky,
Where every tale, every plea, could vie.

The elders listened, their hearts swayed,
By the chorus of voices, not afraid.
Decrees were passed, laws were made,
In the spirit of balance, justice laid.

The city transformed, from silence to song,
Where every voice must fairly belong.
Audi Alteram Partem, the harmony of law,
Ensured justice served as a sharpened saw.

Eldric and Lena, still side by side,
Witnessed the change, their hearts wide.
For in their journey, they had watered,
some treats of shade and fruit that will have
mattered.

"Audi Alteram Partem," the city's new norm,
Certainly a big old welcome reform.
For in the harmony of voices, they had found,
The essence of justice, very much profound.

16. NEMO JUDEX IN CAUSA SUA: No One Should Judge Their Own Cause

Through even darker ravines where Justice's
light dimly shines,
Eldric and Lena pressed on, crossing lines.
To a city where the air, thick with deceit,
Whispered of a trial, much incomplete.

In this place, where fairness rarely did dwell,
Stood a judge, in his own case, a story to tell.
"Nemo Judex in Causa Sua," the old adage rang,
No one to judge their cause, a principle that
sang.

Eldric, with great worry, took to the stage,
Lena by his side, wisdom beyond her age.
Together they stood, before the crowded square,
To challenge injustice, openly laid bare.

"Justice," Eldric began, "demands a blind eye,
To one's own cause, we cannot apply.
For how can fairness truly be,
When the judge and plaintiff are the same
entity?"

Lena, her voice steady and clear,
Added, "This principle we hold dear,
Ensures that every voice is heard fairly,
Under the law, every word treated sincerely."

The judge, cloaked in his own defense,
Felt the weight of their evidence.
For not even power, glory or might,
Could turn the wrong into right.

The city listened, as the duo spoke,
Their words, like a mirror, the illusion broke.

For justice to thrive, to rule the land,
Impartiality must always stand.

So the judge was made to release his case to
plead,
Before another, his fate was kept to read.
In this simple act, the city saw,
A natural principle of judicial law.

Eldric and Lena, through many a trial and test,
Proved that some principles stand way above the
rest.
Firmly establishing Nemo Judex In Causa Sua,
As such a notion that none can get outta.

As they left the city, hearts light and free,
They knew how this victory was key.
For in every corner of the land they'd roam,
The principles of justice, they would enthrone.

Their journey continued, under the sun and
moon,
Their bond, their mission, in perfect tune.
For together, they stood against the tide,
With the law as their guide, justice their pride.

17. TERRA NULLIUS: The Land Unclaimed

Beyond the city's now fairer walls,
Just before another night befalls,
Eldric and Lena found their stride,
Into a land where silence had lied.

"Terra Nullius," the land unclaimed,
Or so the powerful falsely proclaimed.
Yet stories of the past did tell,
Of people who in these lands once dwelled.

With bold intent, they sought to right,
The shadows cast by might's false light.
To bring forth truth from the silenced past,
And honor those whose voices were cast.

Eldric spoke, his voice a flame,
"Let's uncover the truth, reclaim the name
Of those who walked these lands before,
Their stories part of the ancient lore."

Lena, with a map of stars and dreams,
Guided their journey through silent screams.
"To the heart of Terra Nullius we head,
To speak for the silent, the unheard," she said.

They journeyed deep, where the rivers sing,
To a place where the past still clings.
There, they found, hidden by layers of thick
dust,
The remnants of the old, in the earth's crust.

With each step, each discovery made,
The land's true story began to cascade.
Eldric and Lena, with hands entwined,
Wove the tale of those left behind.

"To say this land belongs to no one,"
Eldric cried under the setting sun,

"Is to deny the history, the pain,
Of those who will not walk here again."

Lena gathered the earth, the air, the fire,
Her voice carrying the forgotten choir.
"This land remembers, it knows its own,
And in its memory, the truth is sown."

From Terra Nullius, a lesson learned,
Of respect that must be earned.
For every land has its own song,
A history to which it belongs.

Eldric and Lena, with the truth unveiled,
Showed that justice, though often assailed,
Stands firm when hearts are bold,
And in its grasp, the truth takes hold.

As they left the land that whispers names,
Their journey continued, like unending flames.
For each place they walked, each story told,
Brought justice's warmth to the cold.

Terra Nullius, no longer a land unclaimed,
But a testament to the unnamed.
Eldric and Lena, through history's door,
Brought voices back to the fore.

18. ACTUS REUS & MENS REA: The Importance of Intent

In the wake of the lands where silent stories hath bloom,
Eldric and Lena ventured forth, dispelling gloom.
To a town somehow mysteriously shrouded,
Where the line between guilt and innocence was too clouded.

"Actus Reus and Mens Rea," Lena softly mused,
"The deed and the intent, intricately fused.
For a crime to be, both must align,
In the dance of justice, a step so fine."

Eldric nodded, his thoughts in a whirl,
As around them, suspicions began to unfurl.
A theft had occurred, under the moon's pale
light,
But who was the thief that vanished from sight?

The townsfolk whispered, their eyes wide with
fear,
As Eldric and Lena, to the truth, drew near.
"Let us unravel this tangled skein,
And find where the truth does lain."

With careful steps, they traced the night,
Seeking clues in the fading light.
The Actus Reus was clear to see,
A missing jewel, as large as could be.

But the Mens Rea, the intent behind the deed,
Was hidden in shadows, a mystery to read.
Eldric spoke, "Without the intent,
The act alone cannot our judgment cement."

Together, they delved into the hearts of all,
Listening to stories, both big and small.

Until they found, in a quiet space,
A tale of sorrow, a tale of fallen grace.

A young soul, burdened by need,
Took the jewel, but not out of greed.
The intent was pure, to save a life,
Caught in the throes of cruel strife.

Eldric and Lena, before the town's gaze,
Spoke of the deed, in the morning's haze.
"Actus Reus and Mens Rea, together must stand,
Let's not judge on solely what the act may
demand."

Compassion and understanding began to spread,
As the true story was shared and said.
The town united, to right the wrong,
In a chorus of support, a community strong.

The jewel returned, and with a fine the
forgiveness given,
In the light of justice, the shadows riven.
"Actus Reus and Mens Rea," Lena reflected,
"In the heart of law, are deeply connected."

With the mystery solved, and the truth laid bare,
Eldric and Lena left the town's square.
For each place they touched, with their wisdom
and care,

Left a mark of justice, brightly fair.

Through the dance of shadows, and the light of
intent,
Their journey of justice, ever onward went.
For in every heart, and every prayer,
Lies the balance of Actus Reus and Mens Rea.

19. LEX INIUSTA NON EST LEX: An Unjust Law Isn't A Law At All

After the veil of intent had been lifted clear,
Eldric and Lena, with hearts sincere,
Journeyed on, their path set forth,
To fight for a principle of profound worth.

"Lex Iniusta Non Est Lex," Lena deftly spoke,
"A law unjust, is no law, but just a yoke.
For laws are meant to guard, to guide,
Not to suppress, enslave or divide."

In a town where the law was twisted, bent,
To serve a few, their cruel intent,
Eldric and Lena found their latest cause,
To champion justice, without any pause.

A decree had been passed, in the dead of night,
That filled the people's hearts with fright.
It silenced voices, it chained dreams,
Under its rule, despair reigned supreme.

Eldric stood in the town's grand hall,
His voice rising, cutting through the gloomy
pall.
"This law," he declared, "bears no right,
For an unjust law, holds no might."

Lena gathered the stories, the whispers of pain,
Wove them together, a powerful chain.
"To the council," she urged, "we must present,
A case against this law, its unjust intent."

Together they stood, before the council high,
Underneath the wide, open sky.
"Lex Iniusta Non Est Lex," their united plea,
"For justice to thrive, the council must decree."

The council listened, as around them a hush,
Settled softly, like the evening's gentle brush.

The stories of the people, their plight,
Moved the council, to set things right.

The decree was struck, in a moment profound,
As cheers and cries of joy did heartily sound.
The town was freed, from the unjust law's bind,
In their victory, a truth they did find.

"An unjust law, is no law at all,"
Eldric and Lena, standing tall.
For in their journey, through dark and light,
They fought for what was just, for what was
right.

As they left this town too, their spirits aglow,
They knew their progress, was far from slow.
But ahead lay the greatest test,
To challenge Lord Arbitrus, in his nest.

But strengthened they were, by the battles won,
By the hearts united, by the deeds they'd done.
"Lex Iniusta Non Est Lex," a guiding star,
In their quest for justice, near and far.

20. IGNORANTIA JURIS NON-EXCUSAT, IGNORANTIA FACTI EXCUSAT: Ignorance Of Law is Not- Excusable but Ignorance of Fact May Be

Upon a road less traveled, under the heavens so vast,
Eldric and Lena's steps were dutifully cast.

Towards wisdom's keep, where hermits old,
Held secrets of the law, often untold.

"Ignorantia juris non excusat," they learned,
"Ignorantia facti excusat," the tables turned.
For not all errors are the same in sight,
Some born of darkness, some of light.

In the depths of wisdom's ancient hall,
They sought the truth, to free them all.
The hermits spoke, their voices clear,
Of laws and facts, of far and near.

"Eldric's kin, by Arbitrus baned,
For stepping on grounds, sacred, so claimed.
Yet, they had erred not in law's tight grasp,
But in facts obscured, a truth to clasp."

Eldric and Lena, with newfound might,
Saw the path, the fight for right.
"Lord Arbitrus," they declared, "must see,
The difference in errors, let justice be."

With the sages' blessing, they took to the square,
Gathering the masses, from about everywhere.
The truth they shared, sparked a flame,
A popular uprising, in justice's name.

"Join us," cried Eldric, "in our quest,

For fairness, for truth, for what is best.
Not ignorance of law, but fact's mistake,
Let us and our kin's freedom retake."

Lena, with eloquence, wove the tale,
Of errors made, beyond the pale.
"Ignorance of fact, not law, we plea,
Let this truth set them free."

The supporters rallied, their voices one,
Underneath the now setting sun.
Towards Arbitrus's castle, they marched,
For justice, for truth, their hearts arched.

The eve of reckoning, at last, drew near,
Eldric and Lena, without any fear,
Led the throng, a mighty wave,
For justice's call, they were very brave.

"Ignorantia juris non excusat,
Ignorantia facti excusat,"
This chant, a storm, a force of fate,
Had now arrived before Lord Arbitrus's gate.

Now the stage was set, the players ready,
Their resolve firm, their will steady.
For in the morrow's light, they would face,
Lord Arbitrus, ought to go to justice's embrace.

This penultimate chapter closes, with dawn's
first light,
Eldric and Lena, now ready for the fight.
For truth, for justice, for what is right,
They stood prepared, in the fading night.

21. DUE PROCESS: The Final Triumph

In the shadow of tyranny, under Justicia's
watchful eyes,
Eldric and Lena's journey reached its crescendo,
a battle of the wise.
With every ally rallied, every lesson wielded like
a sword,
They prepared to face Lord Arbitrus, to have
their pleas heard and scored.

Upon the stage of destiny, they stood firm and
bold,
Armed with justice's might and tales everyone
now told.
"Due Process," Eldric proclaimed, a beacon in
the night,
"For fairness, for truth, we gather our might."

The topmost court assembled, a mosaic of fate,
Where Eldric's challenges would articulate.
Against Lord Arbitrus, with tyranny's cloak,
They presented their case, stroke by stroke.

Through the labyrinth of law, with diligence
they tread,
Each argument crafted, each evidence spread.
Lena, ever wise, with strategy and grace,
Guided their course through every phase.

The people's voice, once silenced, now rose in a
wave,
A chorus for justice, strong and brave.
Eldric, with the wind of change now at his back,
Led the charge, no courage did he lack.

The trial, a spectacle of ages, a clash of will and
word,
In the heart of Justicia, every whisper was heard.

Lord Arbitrus, cornered by truth's relentless
light,
Faced the verdict of his deeds, his power's
blight.

The judgment was rendered, with due process's
seal,
A victory for justice, for the commonweal.
Eldric's family, once wronged by decree,
Were vindicated, in triumph, finally free.

But the story doesn't end in the quiet after the
storm,
For from the ashes of conflict, new hope was
born.
A revolt not of swords, but of hearts and minds,
Against tyranny's remnants, in all its kinds.

Eldric, the new sage, with Lena by his side,
Became legends of law, in whom people would
confide.
Their tale, a beacon through the passage of time,
A reminder that justice, in the end, will always
climb.

So let this saga be a guide, a lantern in the dark,
Of how the course of law can leave an indelible
mark.
Eldric and Lena, through trials manifold,

In the annals of Justicia, their story be forever
told.

For in the pursuit of justice, they taught us to
believe,
In the power of law, in the relief it can achieve.
Due Process, a part of their legacy, a testament
to their fight,
In the endless quest for justice, for what was
eventually right.

EPILOGUE

Beneath the canopy of Justicia's endless sky,
Where the echoes of our tale gently lie,
Eldric and Lena, now stand side by side,
At this journey's end, with their hearts open
wide.

From lawlessness of every kind, to justice's gate,
Through trials and tales, they've woven their
fate.
"Lex Poetica," is the lore they've spun,

A path of justice, under the all-seeing sun.

With quill and courage, they've fought the fight,
Turning darkness anywhere into dawning bright
light.
Each principle illustrated, a beacon so bright,
Guiding the lost, with noble insight.

Gently, as the stars whisper through the night,
Eldric and Lena, in the soft moonlight,
Reflect on the journey, on every plight,
On how every wrong led them to what's right.

"Through courts and councils, we've made our
plea,
For a world where justice flows, unabashedly
free.
With every argument, every decree,
We've sown the seeds of what's to be."

In the heart of Justicia, they've carved their
names,
Not just in stone, but also in the flames
Of truth, of justice, of enduring claims,
That in the law, no tyranny reigns.

Now, as they turn, to paths anew,
Under the skies of a brighter hue,
Eldric and Lena, through and through,

Have shown what faith in law can eventually do.

So let their story be a guiding light,
A tale of how to stand for what's right.
For in the end, it's not just about the fight,
But about bringing justice into sight.

"Lex Poetica," more than just a lore,
A testament to what we stand for.
Eldric and Lena, shall be forevermore,
Symbols of the justice we so adore.

As this story closes, let it be known,
In the garden of justice, the seeds have grown.
For the tales of Eldric and Lena have clearly
shown,
A forest of righteousness, now fully blown.

Let us now gather close, as we bid adieu,
To Eldric and Lena, whose hearts were true.
In "Lex Poetica," their journey, a cue,
That justice, in the end, will always renew.

TRIVIA

1. Meaning and Significance of the Name "Eldric": The name "Eldric" is derived from old English elements meaning "old" and "ruler" or "power." In the context of "Lex Poetica," Eldric symbolizes wisdom beyond his years and the power of justice. His name reflects his journey to restore balance and fairness in Justicia, portraying him as a ruler not by throne, but by the moral and ethical leadership he embodies.

2. Meaning and Significance of the Name "Lena": "Lena" is a name with roots in various cultures, often associated with the Greek word for "sunlight" or "moonlight," symbolizing illumination and clarity. In the saga, Lena represents the light of wisdom and practical knowledge that guides Eldric through his trials. Her insight shines on the path of justice, helping to clear the shadows of injustice.

3. The Symbolism of Justicia: Justicia is Latin for "justice," serving as the setting for Eldric's journey. This name underlines the thematic heart of the tale, emphasizing the quest for a just society where law prevails over tyranny. The realm itself becomes a character, reflecting the struggles and triumphs of its inhabitants in their pursuit of fairness.

4. The 21 Phases of Eldric's Journey: Each phase of Eldric's journey correlates with an important principle of law and jurisprudence, symbolizing a step towards understanding and implementing justice. Even the age of 21 is often associated with maturity and the beginning of the bearing of responsibilities, as evident by the legal drinking age or marriage age norms in many countries. Thus the number 21 also mirrors Eldric's growth from a novice to a sage of law.

5. The Concept of "Lex Poetica": The phrase "Lex Poetica", meaning Poetic Law, plays on the term "Ars Poetica," which refers to the art of poetry. By substituting "Ars" (art) with "Lex" (law), the title suggests that law, like poetry, is an art form that requires creativity, interpretation, and deep understanding. It portrays the journey of law and justice as not just procedural but as deeply human and inherently poetic.

---------**END**-----------

www.ingramcontent.com/pod-product-compliance
Lightning Source LLC
Chambersburg PA
CBHW061702130726
47996CB00006B/2126